cat

кішка
kishka

rabbit

кролик
krolyk

dog

собака
sobaka

chick

курча
kurcha

duck
качка
kachka

sheep

вівця
vivtsia

goat

коза
koza

pig

свиня
svynia

donkey

віслюк
visliuk

horse

кінь
kin

cow

корова
korova

mouse

миша
mysha

bat

летюча миша

letiucha mysha

bee

бджола
bdzhola

spider

павук
pavuk

fox

лисиця
lysytsia

deer

олень
olen

squirrel

білка
bilka

hedgehog

їжачок
izhachok

owl

сова
sova

frog

жаба
zhaba

snake

змія
zmiia

racoon

ЄНОТ

ienot

parrot

папуга
papuha

toucan

тукан
tukan

alligator

алігатор
alihator

sea turtle

морська черепаха

morska cherepakha

flamingo

фламінго
flaminho

penguin

пінгвін
pinhvin

crab

краб
krab

jellyfish

медуза
meduza

seal

тюлень
tiulen

shark

акула
akula

whale

кит
kyt

orca

косатка
kosatka

starfish
морська зірка
morska zirka

rhinoceros

носоріг
nosorih

panda

панда
panda

monkey

мавпа

mavpa

lion

лев
lev

tiger

тигр
tyhr

elephant

слон
slon